Friends In The Garden

A Family's Journey

Riina Rumvolt Van Rixoort

To my husband Peter,
my rock and my soul mate

Special thanks to Laurie Bender
for her friendship and design work

Copyright © 2010 by Riina Rumvolt Van Rixoort

Introduction

You who dwell in the gardens with friends in attendance, let me hear your voice.
– Song of Solomon, 8:13

oth my mother and mother-in-law resided in Renaissance Gardens in Seabrook Village. They both suffered from Alzheimer's. My mother Edith lived there for a little over three years. My mother-in-law Muriel spent four and a half years there. We visited the ladies very often. We got to know their neighbors, the other residents at Renaissance Gardens – some by face, others my name. We also got to know some of their family members and the caregivers.

Moving a loved one to Skilled Nursing is very hard. The look on the family member's face, usually a son or daughter, was so familiar. Anxiety, fear and despair. What lies ahead?

I wanted to go and hug that person, tell them the journey is most difficult, but they will get through it and there would be wonderful, caring people to help them along the way. Of course, I didn't do that. That would have been intrusive, totally inappropriate and rude.

The purpose of this book, our family's story, is to be that "hug". If this book helps just one individual in their journey, I will have honored by mother's and my mother-in-law's courage and memories.

Edith

Edith was born in Tallinn, Estonia. She was the daughter of an Army Officer and homemaker. She described her childhood as "golden." She attended a private school. At the age of 16, her privileged world was destroyed by World War II. Her father, along with all of the other Estonian Army Officers, was deported to Siberia by the Soviets and executed a year later. Edith and her mother fled Estonia as the German Army was pulling out and taking refugees by ship. They survived the horrors of war: starvation, homelessness, bombings and worse.

From a refugee camp in Geislingen, they moved to a small village in Northern England, Irwell Vale. Edith met her husband Arnold there. They were married in 1951 and had a daughter, Riina.

In 1962, Edith, along with her daughter, husband and mother, immigrated to the United States, settling in Queens in New York City. She worked at Citibank for 25 years as an Operations Clerk and Customer Service Representative before retiring. She and Arnold moved to Claverack, a small town in upstate New York, about 40 miles south of Albany.

Their retirement years were also "golden," until health problems began to take their toll. They moved to Seabrook Village in 2004 to be closer to me and their son-in-law, and for a supportive lifestyle that met their changing needs. Edith passed away in July 2009.

Muriel

uriel was born and raised in Brooklyn, New York. She graduated from Girls Commercial High School. She spent summers with her family at Cliffwood Beach. She met John Van Rixoort of Union Beach in 1941. They were married in Florida in February 1944.

It was a time of war and Staff Sergeant John Van Rixoort was sent overseas in October 1944 to fight in Europe. Their son Peter was born on January 1st and John was killed in action in Belgium during the Battle of the Bulge 15 days later. Muriel was a bride, wife, mother and widow in one year.

She married Carlton Poling in 1949. She was a real estate agent and homemaker. She spent her free time volunteering at the Bayshore Hospital Thrift Shop for over 30 years.

Her second husband Carlton passed away in 1998. She moved in with her son, Pete. As her health continued to decline, she moved to Renaissance Gardens in 2004. Muriel passed away in 2008.

The Move To Renaissance Gardens

The diagnosis of Alzheimer's is absolutely devastating. No cure, no hope, and some medications that may slow its progression. Edith received that diagnosis in 2003. I was attuned to the early symptoms because my mother-in-law Muriel also had Alzheimer's and her illness was more advanced.

It was a Sunday morning in March 2006 when my father called me. Edith had severe stomach pains. Following a day in the Emergency Room, we had a diagnosis – renal cancer. The cancer had apparently not spread and she was cleared for surgery. Following the surgery, the combination of anesthesia, morphine and other pain medication, and her worsening Alzheimer's resulted in startling personality changes.

My dad called me from Edith's hospital room. I could hear her cursing in Estonian in the background. I speak Estonian, but my grandmother and parents obviously never taught me obscenities. I couldn't understand everything she was saying, which was probably a good thing. But I understood enough. My dad conveyed the cleaned-up version to me. I started laughing and told him that I had heard the "original" version.

That was the start of the journey in the Garden, marked by joy and despair, laughter and tears. Following Edith's release from the hospital, she moved to Rehab at Renaissance Gardens. Our expectation was that she would move to Assisted Living. Her worsening dementia was making it very difficult for her husband to continue caring for her in Independent Living.

"You cannot be a caregiver 24/7." Wise words from a former pastor of mine. There comes a point in your loved one's life when she simply needs professional care. There is also peace of mind knowing that your loved one is safe and being taken care of.

But Edith's health needs now required Skilled Nursing. She moved to the same floor as my mother-in-law in Renaissance Gardens. They became "Friends in the Garden."

The Last Lucid Conversation With My Mother

hen it became apparent that Edith would remain in Skilled Nursing, I dreaded telling her. Often, our fears are much greater than reality.

She was resting in bed and we were chatting. I told her that her health was not good and that her husband Arnold was not able to take care of her right now because his health was not good either. She was going to be living here for a while until she got better and there were people here who would help her. She smiled, nodded and said, "I know." She understood! That was the last lucid conversation I had with my mom.

The Puppy Incident

dith was in a wheelchair, but was still mobile. She had a clip attached to her sweater and an alarm would sound when she tried to get up.

I went to visit my mom on a Sunday afternoon and brought our dog, a Silky Terrier name Schuyler (a.k.a. Skyy). I brought Edith to her room, closed the door and let Skyy off his leash. Edith was playing with him and feeding him biscuits. She adored that little dog. Skyy was about a year old and a true terrier – spirited, rambunctious and playful.

He fell asleep by the door, and my mom and I were chatting. Edith's aide walked past the room, saw the door closed, didn't know I was visiting and became alarmed. She didn't knock, but opened the door to be greeted by a barking dog. I'm sure that wasn't what she was expecting. She was clearly startled and backed out of the doorway. She was now running down the hallway followed by Skyy who was followed by me yelling "Skyy stay! Skyy come!" Halfway down the hallway, Skyy stopped, sat down, looked at me as if to say "What am I doing wrong?"

Edith's aide was now safely in the office and I was totally mortified. A nurse came over, and I asked her if I should go and apologize. She said "no," that she would take care of it. I brought Skyy back to Edith's room and put him on his leash. About 10 minutes later, Edith's aide walked down the other side of the hallway and cautiously looked in the door.

That evening, when Arnold came to visit, the aide told him the story and she was laughing. The aide was also one of my mother-in-law's caregivers. She was kind, caring and compassionate. It is the little things that often matter the most. I went to visit Muriel one evening. Her eyes were closed. Knowing that she was Catholic, her aide (the same one Skyy had chased down the hallway) had turned on the television to the Papal Mass being broadcast at that time.

Advanced Directives

As Edith's daughter, I was the Health Care Proxy and had Power of Attorney. My parents and I had the difficult conversation about their wishes for care during their final days about 25 years ago. It was an awful conversation, but so important. As an only child, I knew that someday, I would probably be making those decisions for them. I knew what they wanted and what they didn't want.

Edith was 82 with advanced Alzheimer's and cancer, two fatal illnesses. Her doctor recommended no chemo or radiation following surgery. The right decision was to sign the Do Not Resuscitate (DNR) and Do Not Hospitalize (DNH) orders. She would of course, be hospitalized if she, for example, fell and broke her hip. But right doesn't make it any easier. I was letting my mother die!

I signed the orders. The Nurse Practitioner at Renaissance Gardens was truly special – a unique combination of medical skills and experience, and such kindness and compassion. As I handed her the papers, she said, "The advanced directive is care and comfort."

My mother was dying and I had to accept that. But I wasn't helpless! I could make sure that she was well cared for and I could comfort her. She had done that for me when I was a little girl and now it was my turn to care take of her.

As a family member, you need to be proactive in your loved one's care. Get to know the staff. Attend quarterly care conferences, which are state mandated in New Jersey. If there is a problem, get it resolved. Be polite and reasonable, but also be a strong advocate for your loved one.

Appreciate the caregivers and let them know you value what they do. You are entrusting your loved one to their care. They have a very tough job. Keep your sense of humor and don't be afraid to cry.

Her Devoted Husband

While this journey was most difficult for Edith, it was also very difficult for her husband Arnold. My dad had been Edith's caregiver for longer than I knew. When my parents lived in upstate New York, I would visit them about once a month for the weekend. I noticed some of the early signs of dementia having seen my mother-in-law suffer with Alzheimer's. But I didn't realize the extent of my mom's illness. I would cook dinner, being the "good daughter." My dad would make breakfast. I didn't realize that she could no longer cook.

My husband Pete once told me, "It gets really hard and then it gets easier once someone else is taking care of them." He had been a caregiver for his mom for years until she moved to Renaissance Gardens.

Once Edith moved to Renaissance Gardens, it became easier for Arnold. He knew that she was safe and protected. She was getting the care she needed. He visited her virtually every day, twice a day. Early on, he would read to her in Estonian, which she enjoyed.

He was a loving, devoted spouse whose heart was breaking. The love of his life was slowly slipping away.

It was so endearing to see the love they shared. When Arnold was leaving one evening, he kissed Edith goodbye several times and told her he would see her tomorrow. She looked up at him, smiled and said "One more." He obliged. They were married for 58 years.

Visiting The Ladies

When both my mother and mother-in-law lived in Renaissance Gardens, I would always visit them both. They had known each other at a time when they were both healthier. One Saturday afternoon, my husband Pete and I had gone to visit the ladies. Pete brought his mom to my mom's room for a visit. They both sat in their wheelchairs, talking and laughing. I had absolutely no clue what they were talking about, but they were enjoying the visit and that was all that really mattered.

Alzheimer's robs you of the ability to communicate. But you don't really know what your loved one knows or doesn't know. Therefore, you should assume that they know and understand everything. And every once in a while, the curtain "opens" for a short time. Those are precious moments.

"Little Baby, Little Baby"

My husband Pete accepted the New Jersey Distinguished Service Medal that was posthumously awarded to his father, who was killed in action during World War II, at a ceremony at the Vietnam Veterans Memorial in Holmdel. There was an article in the local weekly newspaper which included photographs of his father and of Pete receiving the medal, and the story of his parents. The article was posted on the bulletin board in Muriel's room.

I was visiting Muriel and her aide asked about the article. I told her Muriel's story and how she was a bride, wife, mother and widow in one year. Muriel's eyes were following me intently, and then she said, "Little baby, little baby." At that moment, she remembered and understood.

Goodbye, Muriel

We instantly recognized the caller ID from Seabrook Village. It was Tuesday afternoon. Muriel could no longer swallow. When we saw her the next day, she was fairly alert. Our last visit with her was on Saturday afternoon. She passed on Saturday night.

The next day we went to Renaissance Gardens to clean out her room. Many of the staff came to her room to see us, express their condolences and share their last conversations with Muriel. She was surprisingly alert and interactive on her last day.

Her son Pete had pre-arranged the funeral. Making funeral arrangements for a loved on who is still alive is awful and very weird. But you make decisions calmly and rationally. When a loved one passes, everything is done and you can focus on important things.

The next few days were somewhat of a blur. I told Pete that I wanted to deliver Muriel's eulogy. I knew most of her life story, but struggled to write the paragraph about who she was. There was a wonderful description of her written by Pete's godfather's son. He had known Muriel since he was a child. "Your mother was one of the most polite and considerate people I knew, and really set a model for many. She had the rare ability to be fun, active and still be 'proper'". I suddenly realized that there was another Muriel that I had never known. When I first met Muriel, she already had Alzheimer's and this horrible disease changes your personality dramatically.

I delivered the eulogy at her funeral mass. My dad was there despite his very limited mobility and the emotional strain of knowing that his wife's journey was the same as Muriel's. Her human journey was over, and she was at peace and at rest.

Falling Off Cliffs

Watching a loved one decline is like falling off a series of cliffs (metaphorically speaking, of course...) You go along with what has become normal. Then something happens – a change in behavior, a new or worsening health problem, crying. Something is different. You feel as if you have fallen off a cliff. You hurt. Then that becomes the new "normal." And so it goes...

Once you begin to understand this, it's just a little easier to deal with the declines.

Having A Conversation With Edith

ow do you have a conversation with your mom who is not lucid? What she was saying made no sense to me. I couldn't just sit there in stony silence, so I learned a few strategies.

I would parrot back parts of what she was saying. "Really, how interesting, you are right..." – little phrases that work. Also, "I'm glad you (fill in the blank)." At times, we would both laugh – what joy!

My husband Pete taught me three key words – repeat, reassure and redirect, the three "Rs" of caregiving for Alzheimer's. Edith would relive her horrific wartime memories It was so gut wrenching to watch. The memories were probably twisted and distorted nightmares. When I went to visit her one lunchtime, she was crying and said, "Did you hear the Reds (Communists) are coming?" I hugged her, told her that she was in New Jersey in America, that she was safe and she just had a bad dream. Then I told her some cute story about our little dog, Skyy. Repeat, reassure, redirect.

It's Not About You

Every time I walked through the front door of Renaissance Gardens, my stomach would be in knots. As I rode the elevator to the fifth floor, I kept reminding myself that I was there to brighten my mom's day. It was about her, not me. I was "Little Miss Sunshine". I walked onto the fifth floor with a big smile on my face, saying "hello" to the residents and staff. Some residents didn't respond. Others smiled and some said "hello" back. "How are you today?" "That's a pretty blue sweater." Talk to the other residents. You will brighten their day even if they don't respond.

Outside every room is a shadow box for photographs. Many family members put photographs of their loved ones when they were younger and healthier. It serves as a powerful reminder that the residents are so much more than elderly, frail individuals with serious health problems.

One of the photographs I remember seeing was a sepia-toned photograph of a young girl in a pretty party dress. That little girl was somewhere inside that elderly resident.

The Beginning Of The End

s Edith's Alzheimer's progressed, she would often sit in an unresponsive, almost catatonic state with her eyes closed. If you put food to her mouth, she would eat it. She was slipping further and further away.

She developed pressure sores. She was very frail and her immune system was weak. She couldn't heal anymore. She was placed on Vicodin, a powerful pain reliever. The medication knocked her out and she became even less alert. But it was about her being as comfortable as possible, not us.

The Christmas Miracle

Edith's birthday was on December 23rd. My dad and I went to visit her to honor her 84 years. Arnold fed her but she sat there with her eyes closed. We brought her back to her room. We had flowers, a gift and cards. We couldn't wake her up and get her to respond. We left feeling very sad. I told my dad that what mattered was that we were there.

The next day was Christmas Eve. My husband Pete and I, along with our dog Skyy drove to Seabrook. We went to visit Edith expecting the same response as the previous day. Arnold had fed her dinner. To our shock and delight, when we got to her room, she was alert, her eyes were open and she was chatty. She kept looking at Arnold saying in Estonian, "He's a good looking boy."

We had a Christmas card and gifts for her. She understood that it was Christmas and she was surrounded by her loving family. That was her last Christmas and our Christmas miracle. On that holy night, God's mysteries are occasionally revealed to us.

I was telling a dear friend the story and she told me her Christmas miracle. Her mother had suffered a stroke and had been in a coma for about a year. It was Christmas Day, and she left her family and friends to visit her mom in the hospital. She kept saying over and over again, "Hi Mom, it's Pam. I love you. Merry Christmas." To her amazement, her mom opened her eyes, said "Hi Pam. I love you. Merry Christmas." Then she lapsed back into a coma.

Christmas miracles and the grace of God! Gifts we will treasure for the rest of our lives.

Hospice – Read The Fine Print

t was time to place Edith in hospice. The word alone is terrifying. Your loved one will be gone in six months. Of course, no one knows how much time any of us have.

For Edith, hospice meant a higher level of care. She had a private aide five days a week for two hours a day. Mornings were difficult times for her. Perhaps it was the disruption of sleep, bathing and dressing that upset her. She had always been a "morning person" but now she was agitated. Her aide was kind and caring. That attention made a big difference.

The hospice case manager gave me a book about hospice and the dying process. I didn't read it. I didn't want to read it. I didn't want to know more about dying. I put the book in a file drawer. That was a big mistake.

The implicit promise of hospice is that your loved one's final days will be as peaceful and pain free as possible. But you also need to understand what hospice will provide and more importantly, what they will not provide. You will be better prepared for the inevitable.

Edith's Last Days

Edith had developed an infection and fever. She was very frail and aggressive treatment would only increase her suffering. When I heard the news, an incredible sadness descended on me. This was the end that I had anticipated for a long time.

I fed her dinner and she ate well. She fell asleep and looked fairly peaceful. I went to see my dad to tell him the news. We hugged each other and cried.

The phone rang at 3:00 am the next morning. Edith was declining rapidly. I called my dad to tell him the news and I drove down to Seabrook. There was virtually no traffic on the Garden State Parkway.

When I got to her room, a hospice nurse was there as well as staff from Renaissance Gardens. Her blood pressure was very low. I kissed her, told her that I loved her and prayed. Her husband Arnold was there too. Her loved ones were with her. Around 5:00 am her pressure started to rise and she rallied. It would be 16 days before she passed.

The hospice nurses were there for the rest of the day, but then they left. Medicare guidelines! I should have read the fine print in the book hospice gave me.

The weekend was filled with anguish. I felt totally helpless and angry. Miscommunication and misinformation made things even worse. Things changed dramatically on Monday. The nurse practitioner changed Edith's morphine prescription, and from that point on, she seemed comfortable. A hospice nurse told me that I could arrange for a private duty caregiver. (Her colleague had told me earlier that I couldn't do that.) Within two hours, there was a Certified Nurse Aide (CNA) with Edith 24 hours a day. I was fortunate to have the financial resources to pay for that care. And my mom deserved that special care. The Renaissance Gardens staff were very attentive and caring, but they also had other residents to care for.

We were surrounded by some of the most wonderful, kind and caring people during the next two weeks. CNAs are very special people. Their work is very demanding and often they receive very little recognition for their work.

I was with my mom for the next two weeks. At times I went to work for a few hours and checked my email at the PC in the Activities Room. I went home in the evening, had dinner with my husband and slept. Her husband Arnold came to visit her a few times. This was too heartbreaking for him.

Hospice told us that sometimes a loved one needs to hear that it is okay to go home. Arnold did that. He was letting go of that which is most precious to him – his wife of 58 years.

Edith's son-in-law came to see her too. My mother-in-law had passed away 10 months earlier in Renaissance Gardens. I know how difficult it was for him to come and see Edith.

Surrounded By Love

Our family is very small, but for two weeks, it grew exponentially. The love, kindness and compassion we received from the Renaissance Gardens staff and hospice was amazing. I was hugged a lot. The Dining Room staff made sure I ate. The social worker made sure I was okay. The chaplains came to visit and pray with us. One of the chaplains sang "Amazing Grace" to my mother. She has a beautiful voice, and it was so moving and powerful.

The Light In The Darkness

I was leaving Renaissance Gardens one evening. There was a large, dark cloud with rays of sunlight streaming through it. I stopped and stared at it. It was so beautiful. Then the clouds parted to reveal the brilliant sunshine. And then the clouds covered the sun again. "I am the light, the truth and the way."

As I walked down the path towards my car, there was a sparrow on the top branch of a tall pine tree singing its heart out. "His eye is on the sparrow and he watches over me." I had such a sense of peace and God's love.

The Last Gift My Mother Gave Me

 made the decision that I would make the best choices at the time and have no regrets. No second guessing myself afterwards.

Hospice told me that some families hold 24/7 vigils and their loved one doesn't want to leave them when they are there. I would go home in the evening because I needed to rest. I don't know if my being with my mom every day caused her to hang on for 16 days without food and four days without water. She had lost her ability to swallow. But I couldn't bear the thought of her feeling that her loved ones had abandoned her. Did she even know I was there? She was heavily sedated but the morphine was keeping her comfortable.

I asked her! I said in Estonian, "Mom, if you can hear me, squeeze my hand." She didn't. Then I said, "Mom, if you can hear me, close your eyes." Her eyes were very glassy and only half open. She wasn't blinking. She fully closed her eyes and opened them. She answered me. She had heard us tell her how much we loved her, she had heard our prayers.

Edith's Final Day – Saturday, July 25th

Every evening when I left Edith, I would pray, "May the Lord bless you and keep you…", tell her that I loved her very much and that it was okay for her to go home to God to rest. That day was the last time I did that. When I left, I asked the nurse to call me when she passed, not when she declined. It was time for me to let go and for Edith to go home.

The phone rang around 11:00 pm. Edith had returned home.

Celebrating Edith's Life

I came to appreciate how helpful it is to pre-arrange funerals. There were still family and friends to notify, and other things to do. There were over 60 people at her memorial service – family, friends and so many of my colleagues. Her son-in-law Pete delivered the eulogy. The memorial service was in English. She was buried in Kensico Cemetery in Westchester where her mother is also buried. The graveside service was in Estonian.

We are not human beings on a spiritual journey, but really are spiritual beings on a human journey. That was the basic premise of the French theologian Teilhard de Chardin. Edith's human journey has ended and she has returned home. Edith was now at peace and at rest.

You Can't Fast Forward The Grieving Process

had lost the mom I knew for most of my life years before she passed. I thought I could "fast forward" the grieving process. You can't!

I was exhausted, had no enthusiasm for anything and was angry. Denial is strange – you don't realize that you are depressed. There were triggers that would leave me sobbing – hearing "Ave Maria," taking the Estonian raisin bread that my mom had taught me to bake out of the oven and other things that evoked a strong, emotional response of both gratitude and sadness. My husband would just hold me. No words were necessary. He had done that throughout this journey – a journey we shared.

Then one morning in December I woke up and felt strange. I felt good!

The New Normal

y dad found his way to grieve. But I think he was comforted by knowing Edith was at peace and at rest. Watching a loved one suffer is, for some, far worse than losing them.

He plays bridge several times a week and always has a woodworking project in progress in the woodshop. I'm very grateful that he lives in Seabrook, where despite his limited mobility, he can do all of these things.

There is also a community that shares his journey. They can empathize and truly understand what he is experiencing. They are also friends in the garden.

Her Presence In The Light

'm not going to try to explain this. There is a certain quality of light outside that I can't describe, but I feel my mother's presence in the light. Real or not, it's very comforting.

I believe that when we pass away, our spirits, our souls, return to our spiritual home – God's kingdom. But I know that our loved ones live on in our hearts and memories.

Made in the USA
Charleston, SC
29 December 2010